Raintree • Chicago, Illinois

MAKE FRIENDS, BREAK FRIENDS

by Peggy Burns

Illustrated by Deborah Allwright

© 2005 Raintree
Published by Raintree, a division of Reed Elsevier Inc.
Chicago, Illinois

Customer Service 888-363-4266

Visit our website at www.raintreelibrary.com

Illustrated by Deborah Allwright
Packaged by Ticktock Media Ltd.
Designed by Robert Walster, BigBlu Design
Printed and bound in China, by South China Printing

09 08 07 06 05
10 9 8 7 6 5 4 3 2 1

Library of Congress Cataloging-in-Publication Data
Burns, Peggy, 1941-
   Make friends, break friends / Peggy Burns.
      v. cm. -- (Kids' guides)
   Includes bibliographical references and index.
   Contents: Making friends -- Different personalities -- Falling out --
Talking it through -- What would you do?
   ISBN 1-41090-571-3 (lib. bdg.)
   1. Child psychology--Juvenile literature. 2. Interpersonal relations
in children--Juvenile literature. 3. Friendship in children--Juvenile
literature. [1. Friendship. 2. Interpersonal relations.] 1. Title. II.
Series: Kids' guides (Chicago, Ill.)
HQ772.5 .B87 2005
155.4'18--dc22
                                    2003021986

Some words are shown in bold, **like this.** You can find out what they mean by looking in the glossary.

CONTENTS

INTRODUCTION

4

Everybody needs friends. It is great to be able to get along with other people and to have friends to play with. When you are unhappy about something, your friends are there to help and give you **advice.** You are there for them, too. Talking to a friend about worries helps everyone to cheer up.

Having friends makes life much more interesting, especially if they have different interests, **talents,** or toys!

Making and keeping friends is not always easy. Some people are friendly and outgoing, while others are **shy** and find it hard to make friends. Some people are easily hurt by teasing and name-calling, while others are able to shrug it off and not let it bother them.

You and your friends will not always agree with each other. That is why friends sometimes **quarrel** and break up. This book should help you when you do. And if you are feeling lonely and want to make friends, there is advice for you, too.

Why can't I make friends easily?

Let's Talk About...
MAKING FRIENDS

It is important to have friends. Some people enjoy having a lot of friends. Other people like to have just one or two close friends. But not everyone finds it easy to make friends. If you are **shy,** you might find it hard to talk to people. But it's not always about being shy. Making friends is sometimes hard for people who are talkative, too!

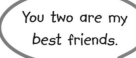

You two are my best friends.

BUT WHY ME?

There can be all kinds of reasons why you might find yourself with no one to play with. Maybe the other children are not very friendly. You may have just moved or started a new school. Whatever the reason, you can do something about it.

If you want to talk to someone, it sometimes helps to think of things you could talk about. Try to find something you have in common. Talking about that could be the start of a great friendship.

Here are some ideas:

● Talk about TV shows, games, or books you enjoy.
● Invite him or her to play your favorite game with you.
● Say you like his or her hairstyle.

WHY DO I FEEL LIKE THIS?

Having no friends can make anyone feel left out and lonely. But try not to look too sad. When you look happy and friendly, it is easier for other people to come talk to you.

LOOK AT IT ANOTHER WAY

It is easy to **resent** it when other people don't talk to you or leave you out of their games. But if you are shy and quiet, they may hardly know you are there. Don't wait for others to smile at you, smile at them first.

Let's Talk About...

DIFFERENT PERSONALITIES

People come in all shapes and sizes and colors, and they all have different **personalities.** People can be cheerful or moody, kind or mean, generous or selfish. They have ideas, **opinions,** and feelings of their own. You can learn a lot by listening to other people. But however hard you try, you are not likely to get along with everybody.

BUT WHY ME?

If someone is being unkind to you, you have every right to feel angry or upset. But people have their own reasons for arguing or pouting. It helps to know why friends act like they do.

One minute you are playing happily together, the next, your friend is in a bad mood. It is all very confusing! You may be left wondering what you have said or done to upset your friend. Or you might simply feel angry or worried.

Everyone has bad times when they feel unhappy. You might have friends who are happy and nice most of the time, but when things don't go their way they say nasty things, or pout and won't talk to you. Being ignored can be just as awful as being yelled at.

Here are some things you can do:
- Talk to your friend.
- Try to understand why he or she acts in an unkind way.
- Explain how hurt and upset you get when you are treated poorly.

LOOK AT IT ANOTHER WAY

Maybe your friend has not stopped to think how he or she makes you feel. Getting mad might just be a **bad habit,** and bad habits can be changed.

Let's Talk About...
FALLING OUT

When you are mad at someone it is easy to let your feelings take over. You start shouting, your friend shouts back. You both may say things you don't mean. Before you know it, you've stopped being friends. Arguments often start when you and your friend are kidding around and teasing each other. Sometimes teasing can get out of hand. Suddenly it is not fun anymore.

BUT WHY ME?

Teasing can start for all sorts of reasons. Maybe because you are tall or short, or because you are **shy** or loud. It helps to know why a friend is being nasty to you, so ask them and tell them how you feel.

Most of the time teasing is just friends having fun together. But teasing can sometimes turn nasty. If you don't enjoy your friend's teasing, here are some things you can do:

- Tell your friend how you feel.
- If it happens again, firmly tell your friend to stop it.
- Don't bottle up your feelings for long. Tell someone.

WHY DO I FEEL LIKE THIS?

Sometimes the things your friends say make you feel silly or stupid, especially when others are listening. Being treated this way makes you feel bad, and it is not your fault!

LOOK AT IT ANOTHER WAY

There are always reasons why people say hurtful things. Your friend could just be **thoughtless** and not realize that he or she is hurting your feelings. But there are people who enjoy hurting others. Sometimes it is because they themselves are being picked on.

MISTER BOSSY

Hi there. I'm Lewis, and I'm going to be a soccer player one day! At school I play with my friends during breaktime. Some of them are pretty good, and some aren't. For instance, Jack likes to play, but he misses every ball.

Yesterday Jack wanted to play, but I told him he was no good and that he'd spoil the game. Derek stuck up for him. He said it wasn't just my game. So I walked off and let them play by themselves.

Now I am standing on the sidelines watching.
I thought they would play a bad game without
me, but they're not. They're even laughing and
joking. I don't know what to do.

MISTER BOSSY — Talking It Through

It helps to talk to someone...

A TEACHER

Lewis's teacher, Mr. Graham, comes over. He says that if Lewis wants to play professionally one day he needs to learn to be part of a team. He cannot always make himself the team captain.

A FRIEND

Derek tells Lewis that he shouldn't tell people they're not any good. Instead, he should help them. Jack looked hurt and upset when Lewis told him he could not join in. How is Jack going to improve if he cannot play?

A PARENT

Lewis's mom says she is proud he is so good at soccer and that he is a natural leader. Maybe one day he will be the captain of his own team. But he needs to learn that bossy leaders are not good leaders.

FORWARD STEPS

• LISTEN

Pay attention to good advice, even when people tell you things you don't like to hear.

• ENCOURAGE OTHERS

Be a good team player by helping others to learn.

I didn't enjoy watching my friends play soccer without me, and I realized how Jack must have felt. It's awful being left out. I talked things over with a few people. My mom seems to think I'm a bit bossy. Maybe she's right!

Today I told Jack I was sorry and we all played together. Jack really wants to learn to play better. He asked me to show him how to trap the ball. Derek was right, I can help Jack improve.

I decided that from now on I'm going to be a real team player instead of always wanting to be the boss.

True Stories

SHE LOOKS DIFFERENT

My name's Amy, and I go to elementary school. When we went back after spring break a new girl named Maura was sitting next to me. The first thing I noticed was that Maura's face was all patchy and shiny and scarred. I heard some people behind us whispering about her.

What's with the new girl, Amy?

Gosh, look at her face.

It looks really freaky!

Maura saw me looking at her, and she gave me a nasty look before turning her head away. I thought, well if she doesn't want to be friendly, that's fine by me! I didn't talk to her all day, even though Mrs. Johnson had asked us to be nice to her.

But at playtime the next day, some people in my class started to tease Maura and say nasty things. I feel really bad for not being nice yesterday and now I feel sorry for her. I don't know what to do!

SHE LOOKS DIFFERENT

Talking It Through

It helps to talk to someone...

A BIG SISTER

Amy's sister is sad when Amy tells her about Maura's scarred face. She says, "You should try to forget the way Maura looks. It's what people are like on the inside that really matters."

A TEACHER

Mrs. Johnson says that nobody deserves to be teased or bullied because they look different. But she is glad that Amy can see that for herself. Now she can really help Maura settle in.

A GRANDPARENT

Amy's grandma says she should try to understand how Maura feels when people stare at her. No wonder Maura turned away and seemed unfriendly. She probably just wants to be treated like anyone else.

FORWARD STEPS

● **TALK**

Take the trouble to find out what people are really like.

● **UNDERSTAND**

It is what a person is like on the inside that matters.

The next day, I smiled at Maura and said "hello." At lunch we started to talk. She told me that she had been burned in a house fire and the burns had made scars that will never go away.

She said she used to be quite pretty. She's had **operations** on her face, but the doctors won't be able to make her look like she used to. I felt bad when I remembered how I'd ignored her. I said sorry because I just hadn't understood.

Maura said it was all right. She even shared her homemade cookies with me. The next day I told my friends about it so they could start to see how nice she is. Now we're all friends and don't even notice her burns!

True Stories

I LIED

Hi, I'm Keeley. I did a silly thing recently, and now I feel **embarrassed** even thinking about it. I think it happened because nobody ever seemed to notice me any more.

My mom and stepdad Steve are expecting a baby. All they talk about are cribs, diapers, car seats, and whether to paint the baby's room pink or blue.

You'd think I was invisible.

Even at school I'm just one of the crowd, and no one special. So one day I told my best friend Bridget that my mom had been rushed to the hospital, really sick. Before long everybody was fussing over me. All my friends felt sorry for me. It felt good to be noticed for once!

We heard about your mom...

Are you okay?

And then Bridget saw me and Mom at the supermarket, and she knew I'd been telling lies. I feel awful and I don't know what to do.

I LIED Talking It Through

It helps to talk to someone...

A STEPPARENT

Keeley's stepdad says he is sorry for being so **preoccupied** with the baby. He's happy that she told him how she feels. He promises to start taking her swimming again on the weekends, like he always used to do.

A PARENT

Mom reminds Keeley that she loves her very much and the baby will never take her place. She says she can understand why Keeley wants attention, but it is never good to lie. Keeley should tell the truth.

A FRIEND

Bridget is a little angry about it because she and Keeley are best friends. She says that Keeley should have told her how she was feeling, and now she should tell everyone that she is sorry.

FORWARD STEPS

- **BE CONFIDENT**

  Value yourself for the special person you are.

- **TELL THE TRUTH**

  If you have made up stories that aren't true, talk to your friends and tell them why. Don't forget to say "sorry!"

I was **ashamed** of making up that silly story, so I took Bridget's advice and told everyone in my class that I was really sorry for telling lies. When I explained why it had happened, they understood.

Mom and Steve **apologized.** They said they'd been so excited about the baby, they hadn't thought that I might be feeling left out. We all went swimming on Saturday and then had burgers and ice cream. After that they bought me a cute new top and they let me choose the color for the baby's room.

So everything turned out okay. But I have decided that I'm never going to tell lies to my friends again. It's not worth it!

I WISH THEY'D STOP

24

Hi there. My name is Kessar. That is my real name anyway. Because I am a little overweight, my friends Charles and John call me Tubs. I know they are only teasing. They don't mean to be nasty, but it sometimes makes me feel fat and ugly.

I don't like them calling me Tubs. I wish they'd stop.

We all belong to a swimming club at the local pool. I love swimming, but wearing a swimsuit makes them tease me even more. A few weeks ago I jumped in off the top board and made huge waves that splashed everyone. My friends didn't say much, they just laughed. But I knew exactly what they were thinking.

I've seen whales make smaller splashes!

Hee, hee. Nice one, Tubs.

I've decided not to go swimming any more. At least, not until I get a little slimmer. I am trying!

I WISH THEY'D STOP

Talking It Through

It helps to talk to someone...

A CLUB LEADER

Mr. Walker advises Kessar to tell his friends how he feels. He reminds Kessar that swimming is a good way to exercise, and will help him to keep fit and lose weight.

A PARENT

Kessar's dad tells him not to worry about his looks and to enjoy his time at the pool. He says that if Kessar is worried about his weight, though, he could stop having french fries on his way home every day!

A FRIEND

Charles says he had no idea how Kessar was feeling. He tells Kessar that he would really miss him at the club. He says Kessar is a good swimmer and he shouldn't quit because of a silly name.

FORWARD STEPS

- ### VALUE YOURSELF
  You're important just as you are!

- ### HAVE FUN, BE NICE
  It's never right to call people names or make fun of them *because of the way they look.*

Charles was really surprised when I told him how I felt, and he told John. They said it was just a nickname, and they hadn't realized it upset me. They promised to stop calling me Tubs. John said the swimming club wasn't the same without me, and asked me to come back.

I took my friends' **advice** and started going to the club again. These days I'm trying to forget about my size and focus on being a better swimmer. Mr. Walker's right. People who want to lose weight need exercise, and swimming is exercising and having fun at the same time!

Charles and John did stop calling me Tubs. I know now that good friends care about each other and try not to hurt their friends' feelings.

Quiz

WHAT WOULD YOU DO?

1. What would you do if people noticed that you always wanted to be in charge, like Lewis, and they started calling you bossy?

a)   Tell them firmly to mind their own business.

b)   Let them play without you to teach them a lesson.

c)   Tell a teacher that your friends are picking on you.

d)   Stop making all the decisions and give other people a chance to lead.

2. What would you do if, like Amy, you met someone who looked different?

a)   Ask what's wrong with the person.

b)   Treat the person as you would anyone else.

c)   Sympathize with the person and say how sorry you are.

d)   Don't talk to the person, because he or she might not be nice.

3. What would you do if, like Keeley, you wanted to make people believe stories about you that weren't true?

a)   Tell them if you want to, because making up stories isn't like telling real lies.

b)   Don't worry about it, because everyone tells lies anyway.

c)   Think of your own good points and decide that you don't need to tell lies about yourself.

d)   Decide that it's okay to tell lies as long as you don't get caught.

4. What would you do if, like Kessar, you didn't like the way your friends teased you?

a) Ignore it because they might stop hanging out with you if you tell them how you feel.

b) Start teasing them too, and see how they like it.

c) Forget about it. It's okay for friends to tease each other.

d) Tell them it hurts when they call you names, even in fun.

Answers

1. d) Remember that your friends also need to learn how to be leaders!

2. b) People who look different in some way, like having scars or a birthmark, are just the same as anyone else.

3. c) You don't need to make up stories about yourself. Telling lies to your friends could make them angry or distrust you.

4. d) Always tell people how you feel. If you are hurt by the unkind things people say, that's not teasing, it's bullying. Bullying is always wrong.

Glossary

advice   when someone helps you to decide what to do or say

apologize   say "sorry"

ashamed   knowing that you have done something wrong and feeling bad about it

bad habit   something bad you do all the time without thinking about it

embarrassed   when you feel awkward and your face turns red

operations   something done by doctors in hospitals to try to make a person healthier

opinions   things that you believe in or feel strongly about

personality   way you think and behave

preoccupied   distracted and not focusing on something

quarrel   argument or disagreement

resent   feeling angry about something you feel is unfair

shy   not sure of yourself, not outgoing

talents   things you do well, such as football, drawing, or swimming

thoughtless   not thinking about whether things you do or say will affect other people

More Books to Read

Feeney, Kathy. **Feel Good.** Mankato, Minn.: Capstone, 2000.

Frost, Helen. **Feeling Angry.** Mankato, Minn.: Capstone, 2000.

Frost, Helen. **Feeling Happy.** Mankato, Minn.: Capstone, 2000.

Frost, Helen. **Feeling Sad.** Mankato, Minn.: Capstone, 2000.

Lovitt, Chip. **Sharing.** Vero Beach, Fl.: Rourke, 1999.

Maurer, Tracy. **A to Z of Friends and Family.** Vero Beach, Fl.: Rourke, 2001.

Powell, Jillian. **Bullying.** Chicago: Raintree, 1999.

Ross, Dave. **A Book of Friends.** New York: HarperCollins, 1999.

Suben, Eric. **Friendship.** Vero Beach, Fl.: Rourke, 1999.

Waters, Jennifer. **Be a Good Friend!** Minneapolis: Compass Point, 2002.

Index